Contents

What is light?

Light lets us see things.

Light bounces off things and passes into our eyes. This is how we can see things.

Sources of light

light

light

Light comes from different places.

We call these sources of light.

Sources of light make their own light.

If an object does not make light, it is not a source of light.

Sunlight

Sun

The Sun makes its own light.

Sunlight is very bright.

Never look straight at the Sun.

It is so bright it can hurt your eyes.

Starlight and moonlight

A star makes its own light.

Stars twinkle in the night sky.

The Moon does not make its
own light.

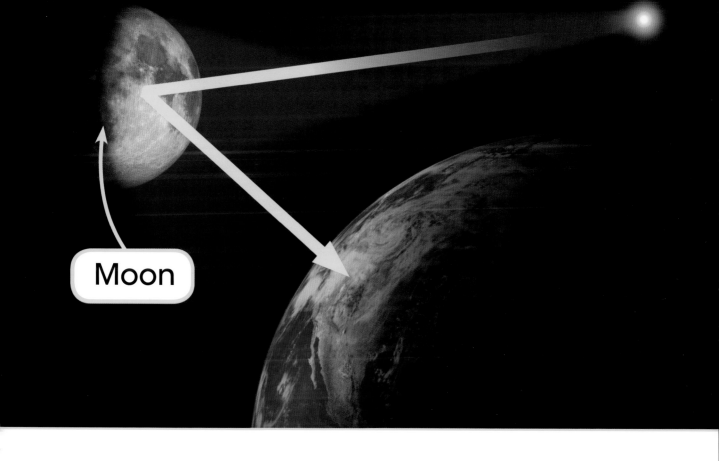

Moon

The Moon reflects or bounces light from the Sun.

Light made by people

Some sources of light are made by people.

A light bulb makes light using electricity.

flame

A candle makes light using a flame.

Traffic lights and televisions are sources of light, too.

Spot the sources of light

Three of these things are sources of light. Can you spot them?

Answer on page 24

Picture glossary

electricity a form of energy used to make light bulbs work

Moon a large object in space that goes around our planet

reflect when light bounces off the surface of an object

Sun the star closest to Earth

Index

Answer to question on page 22
The three sources of light are: the Sun, the traffic lights, and the torch.

Notes for parents and teachers

Before reading

Explain to the children that light comes from sources of light. Ask them to look around the room and identify as many sources of light as possible. Are there any that they missed? Or any that are NOT sources of light? Can they distinguish sources of light made by people and natural sources of light? Which do they think is the most important (i.e., the Sun)?

After reading

- Shine a torch onto a mirror. Ask the children if they can identify any sources of light. If anyone suggests the mirror, explain that the mirror is not itself a source of light, but rather is reflecting light from the torch.

- Ask the children if they can think of any objects in the sky that are sources of light (the Sun, the stars). The Moon is NOT a source of light. In fact it is acting like the mirror in the first example – it is reflecting the light of the Sun.